PRAYER, MYSTERIES, AND RELATIONSHIP.

PAIGE WILLIAMS

CONTENTS

FOREWORD

In 2020, Paige Williams received a word and a dream from Jesus regarding my life after just meeting him one time. These two words, along with the Trinity, have since transformed my life into an epicenter for the supernatural. These words released things in my daily life that would take too long to write, but to name a few; I have heard the voice of God audibly, Jesus has visited me, and my wife has had countless dreams come to pass in the two years that Paige has mentored us. I have had the great pleasure of doing ministry with Paige since this time and there has not been a time when he gets done speaking that the people aren't astonished at his teachings (Matthew 7:28-29). There was one time while driving home the Lord spoke to me and told me that there was no one else on Earth that has the revelation that Paige had because he got it directly from Him & Father in the secret place.

Galatians 1:12 *I received my message from no human source, and no one taught me. Instead, I received it by direct revelation from Jesus Christ.*

The above verse is the epitome of Paige's secret life spent in the secret place, and whatever is written in the pages of the book you are about to read, no one has ever spoke these things in the way that you will read here. Much of it Father has hidden away, set aside for Paige to discover and then bring to you for such a time as this (Proverbs 25:2). This book will astonish you, it will reveal secret treasures, and it will peel back any residual of the veil between the natural and the supernatural in your walk on Earth.

I pray in the name of Jesus that God will bear witness to the truths found here through intense visitation, miracles, and dreams. I pray the Spirit opens your ears to the truth, and that He hones your eyes in on the prize. Holy Spirit, have your way with this reader, give them the fullness of the meat hidden in this book, and fill them with understanding and awe. Father, I pray that the door to the secret place appears more inviting than it ever was for this reader, and that you would show them the wonder that is your Kingdom. Amen.

Jake Richards
Director of Community and Listener Engagement
YES FM Radio Ministries
Founder of Light The Fire Revival Conference

INTRODUCTION

I am excited to release the revelations that the Lord has given me for this time and season. It's not by coincidence but it's by instruction that I'm releasing this book at this time. There is fresh manna from God contained in the pages of this book that will help sustain everyone who reads it in the days ahead. You will be able to come back to this book and be refreshed and edified by what The Spirit is saying through its pages. God told me this book is a *sustainer*. To sustain is to keep from falling, to bear, to uphold, to support as a foundation sustains a superstructure. This book will accomplish all of that and more, because this book is *supernatural* (meaning it's from Heaven). This book, like manna from Heaven will keep your spirit nourished for seasons at a time and help you to be strong in Him, especially against the attacks of the enemy. *The Lord also Promised He would walk the pages of this book with every reader and open heart to Bless them with His Glory!* Now let's begin!

ABRAHAM THE PATRIARCH OF GRACE

Have you ever heard the saying *"To understand where you're going, you have to understand where you've been?"* This is also true in the spiritual sense. If we're to understand where we're going spiritually we have to understand where we've been spiritually. We need to know our spiritual history and lineage. The Bible says that Abraham is our spiritual father and that we have a spiritual inheritance through his faith in God.

Galatians 3:7 KJVS

*[7] Know ye therefore that they **which are of faith**, the same are the **children of Abraham**.*

Galatians 3:29 KJVS

*[29] And if **ye be Christ's**, then **are ye Abraham's seed**, and **heirs** according to the promise.*

We see here through these scriptures that through our faith in Christ Jesus, we receive the blessings and inheritance of Abraham. But many of us Christians are highly unfamiliar with what that really means, entails, and provides for us. But that soon will change...just keep reading!

First, we have to understand that Abraham was a forerunner and patriarch of Grace. He was the first to experience the Covenant of Grace, that would come through Jesus Christ thousands of years later. He lived before the law was given and was made a partaker of the better Covenant. And was justified by His faith in what God had revealed to him and was counted as righteous by God.

Romans 4:3 KJVS

[3] For what saith the scripture? **Abraham believed God**, *and it was* **counted unto him for righteousness.**

This is the first benefit of Grace, that we are counted as righteous or right with God through faith alone in Him! But the Bible also says in Romans 10:17 *"So then* **faith cometh by hearing, and hearing by the word of God.**" So our father Abraham could not have had faith unless the Word of God was preached to him. Because according to this scripture if there is no word from God, there is no faith! Here is the scripture to support this statement:

Galatians 3:8-9 KJVS

[8] **And the scripture**, *foreseeing that* **God** *would justify the heathen through faith,* **preached before the gospel unto Abraham,** *saying, In thee shall all nations be blessed. [9] So then* **they which be of faith are blessed with faithful Abraham.**

We see right here that the Gospel was preached to Abraham by God *before* Christ came in the flesh. He received the Gospel of Jesus Christ prior to Him coming to earth. That's amazing! Jesus spoke of Abraham having insight and revelation into His life and dispensation.

John 8:56 KJVS

[56] Your father **Abraham rejoiced to see my day:** *and* **he saw it, and was glad.**

Abraham had a revelation of Grace that was literally before his time. But to be a father and pass down an inheritance, you must experience and obtain it first, before your children can experience and obtain it.

Galatians 3:14 KJVS

[14] That the **blessing of Abraham** *might come on the* **Gentiles**

*through Jesus Christ; that we might **receive the promise of the Spirit through faith.***

Did you know that Pentecost and the outpouring of God's Spirit is a part of our inheritance as the children of Abraham by faith? That Jesus activates this Covenant that God made with Abraham in our lives the day we repent and come to faith in Him? *It's true!*

To further understand what is available to us through the blessing of Abraham we have to take a closer look at his life and what he experienced.

First Abraham was a spiritual emperor, he was called to give birth to kings!

Genesis 17:5-6 KJVS

*[5] Neither shall thy name any more be called Abram, but thy name shall be Abraham; for a father of many nations have I made thee. [6] And I will make thee exceeding fruitful, and I will make nations of thee, and **kings shall come out of thee.***

To understand what God was saying to Abraham we have to understand royal rank and order. Kings give birth to *princes* but emperors give birth to *kings*! Jesus Himself being an Emperor activated this royal inheritance from Abraham through His Blood.

Revelation 1:5-6 KJVS

*[5] **And from Jesus Christ**, who is the faithful witness, and the first begotten of the dead, and the **prince of the kings of the earth**. Unto him that loved us, and washed us from our sins in **his own blood**, [6] And hath **made us kings** and priests unto God and his Father; to him be glory and dominion for ever and ever. Amen.*

Jesus being called the prince of the kings of the earth is another way of calling Him an emperor. It states that He has rulership over all the kings of the earth, which is the seat of an emperor. Abraham also was an emperor called to give birth to kings by God. So to be a child of Abraham makes you a king through the Blood of Jesus! And being a king means that we have a kingdom over which to rule with dominion, and authority to govern it. Now because we are kings and of royal descent, we now have access to Fellowship with the King of kings and The Lord God Almighty. We now have inherited the opportunity to be *His friend*, like our spiritual father Abraham.

To understand the value and privilege of this, we must understand kingdom protocol and order. In a kingdom commoners or what we would call normal people are not allowed or permitted to be in the king's presence directly. You must be a royal or in the king's royal court to access him rightfully. So what our Lord Jesus did on the cross, making us kings through the blessing and inheritance of Abraham, has given us legal access to God. It grants us the high privilege and honor to be and dwell in His Throne Room and in His Royal Courts. This in turn gives us the opportunity through access to God to be His friends! You cannot be someone's friend if you are not able to spend quality time with them or even have access to be close to them. Jesus did this by His Blood and by instituting the Covenant God made with Abraham to all who would believe in Him. Through the Blessings of Abraham instituted by The Lord, we have royal access and opportunity to be as close to God as we desire to be!

Now what was Abraham's Fellowship like with the Lord? Let's see! Abraham had a Fellowship with arguably the most mysterious man in the Bible, his name is Melchisdec. Let's take a look at his description in the Bible.

Hebrews 7:1-4 KJVS

[1] For this Melchisedec, king of Salem, priest of the most high God, who met Abraham returning from the slaughter of the kings, and blessed him; [2] To whom also Abraham gave a tenth part of all; first being by interpretation King of righteousness, and after that also King of Salem, which is, King of peace; [3] Without father, without mother, without descent, having neither beginning of days, nor end of life; but made like unto the Son of God; abideth a priest continually. [4] Now consider how great this man was, unto whom even the patriarch Abraham gave the tenth of the spoils.

So we see that this Melchizedek was a king and a priest of God. Who also had authority to bless Abraham. And the scripture says:

Hebrews 7:7 TPT

*[7] And no one could deny the fact **that the one who has the***

power to impart a blessing is superior to the one who receives it.

This tells us that Melchizedek was superior or greater than Abraham because He was the one imparting the blessing to Abraham, and not the other way around. We also see through the previous scripture that Abraham paid tithes to this man, which is reserved for *God*. Melchizedek was indeed another manifestation of Christ, in a way that Christ could be revealed through his form, while yet being hidden until the appointed time of his birth. But we're not here to talk about Melchisedek...back to Abraham! But I will confirm this principle of Christ appearing in *another form* through scripture.

Mark 16:12 KJVS

*[12] After that **he appeared in another form unto two of them**, as they walked, and went into the country.*

Our father Abraham became a first partaker of the *Imperial priesthood* that is found in Jesus Christ before the dispensation of Grace. What he experienced was greater than the law because it was before the law. He was a first partaker of the Covenant of Grace. Abraham also received the first recorded Face to face appearance in the flesh from the Lord Jesus in the Bible. That is a Grace experience! Abraham was actually operating in *dominion over time!* His dominion over time was also revealed in the miraculous birth of his son to his elderly wife Sarah, which was a revelation that Abraham had dominion over *time*. Abraham time traveled into the dispensation of Grace in his day and time. He jumped into a privilege not yet afforded to man on the earth in his time, through the Credit of Christ's Blood which was shed before the foundation of the world according to Revelation 13:8. That is why in the book of Romans and Hebrews his life is taught as an example of how to live successfully in the dispensation of Grace. Abraham was justified by faith just like the new Covenant believer. Abraham also took part in the communion, or last supper experience in Genesis 14:18 before the time of Christ. I *must* mention Melchizedek at this time for revelation purposes, to understand that Abraham was in fact having fellowship with Jesus Christ Himself.

Hebrews 7:2-3 KJVS

[2] To whom also Abraham gave a tenth part of all; first being

*by interpretation **King of righteousness**, and after that also **King of Salem**, which is, **King of peace**; [3] Without father, without mother, without descent, having neither beginning of days, nor end of life; but made like unto the Son of God; abideth a priest continually.*

The name King of Righteousness can actually be interpreted in the original language as King of Justification. Which we now know is the Lord Jesus Christ the Son of God!

Galatians 3:8 KJVS

*[8] And the scripture, foreseeing that **God would justify the heathen through faith, preached before the gospel unto Abraham**, saying, In thee shall all nations be blessed.*

Galatians 3:24 KJVS

*[24] Wherefore the law was our schoolmaster to **bring us unto Christ, that we might be justified by faith.***

Romans 5:1 KJVS

*[1] Therefore being **justified by faith, we have peace with God through our Lord Jesus Christ:***

So through these scriptures we realize that Jesus is the King of Justification to all those who put their faith in Him. Also that because of Him we have *peace* with God our Father, through his blood. So we see that the names King of Righteousness and Peace are revelation names of the Lord Jesus Christ. It should also be noted that the word *Salem* in the name King of Salem is the abbreviated way of saying Jerusalem, and we all know that Jesus Christ is the King of Jerusalem, the King of the Jews!

Micah 7:20 KJVS

*[20] Thou wilt perform the truth to Jacob, **and the mercy to Abraham**, which thou hast sworn unto our fathers from the days of old.*

God gave Abraham the mercy or lovingkindness of Grace before the fullness of its dispensation. So that we would have an earthly father to inherit this from through faith in Jesus!

There is a special revelation and mystery that is revealed about the life of Abraham in the book of Jasher mentioned in Joshua 10:13 and 1 Samuel 1:18. It is written in Jasher 12:22-25. It speaks of Abraham (then Abram) being thrown into a fiery furnace and not being consumed! For Bible readers this scenario sounds very familiar. It happened in the book of Daniel to the three Hebrew boys who wouldn't worship the king's image. So in light of this revelation, we see that the three Hebrew boys' experience was in fact an inheritance or blessing from father Abraham. The supernatural provision of God not to be consumed! We too have this same inheritance. We may not be thrown in a literal fiery furnace but life itself and the attacks of the enemy can be our fiery furnace. But you and I have a rich inheritance through our father Abraham not to be consumed but preserved by God no matter what! That's a glorious thing!

THE LOVE OF ABRAHAM AND ISAAC

There is a mystery and revelation in the relationship and sacrifices of Abraham and Isaac that many have overlooked. This mystery and revelation will prove to be vital to your relationship and friendship with God. It will also enlighten you to the Love Dimensions of God.

When God spoke to Abraham and commanded Him to sacrifice his son Isaac, He was inviting Abraham into the depths of His Heart. To something so personal and mysterious that it would continue to unfold for thousands of years. But the heart of it was revealed to Abraham when he *obeyed God*, which is to *love God!* God was actually inviting Abraham into a personal fellowship with Him. One that only a *father* could understand. And not just any father, but a father sacrificing the life of their son!

The mystery in this invitation of God to Abraham is that he was becoming one with the Heart of God. *Which is to love someone enough to sacrifice (kill) your son for them!* God desired someone to know Him in that dimension and capacity, and he chose Abraham. Who was a true father, to know Him in that way. To know the pain, hurt, sacrifice and deep love of sacrificing the most precious person you have for someone else you love!

This was not the only love that was manifested on that day. There was not only the love of the father but *the love of the son!* Which is to do the Will of your father and become the sacrifice, laying down your life because of the father's love for someone else. Isaac was willing to lay down his life for his father's devotion to God. Just as Christ was willing to lay down His Life because of His Father's Devotion to us. You see, the love of The Father and The Son were depicted in this one act of Abraham and Isaac. They were symbolically revealing the future and the love that had to manifest for it to take place. *It was the Love of Relationship between The Father and The Son!*

We must understand that it's the relationship between a father and a son that saves the world! When a deep and loving relationship is established between a father and a son it saves generations and multiple others who come in contact with them. The relationship between a husband and a wife gives birth to *new life,* but the relationship between a father and a son *shaped and continues to shape the future!* When the church (bride) is in union with Christ (the Bridegroom) it gives birth to new life or what we call salvation. But it was the Love between The Father and Jesus The Son that changed the world and the course of humanity. This is why the Apostle John said this by The Spirit:

1 John 3:1 KJVS

*[1] Behold, what manner of love the Father hath bestowed upon us, **that we should be called the sons of God...***

The relationship between a father and a son gives direction to the life that a husband and wife gives birth to! The creation cries out for sons, because mature sons change the future! The only way sons can mature is through a deep relationship with a father. This explains the lack of truly mature men in the times we live in. If there were deep relationships with mature fathers, it would breed maturity in sons! But because many times this is not the case, there is a lack of maturity in men, especially in America. Now I did not say father's weren't there or in the home (and we know some are not) but that they were not mature. You see, it is God's design that son's are matured by a mature natural father as well as by Himself. The sad truth is that many fathers are not there to raise their sons, or they are not mature enough to breed or sow maturity into their sons. Fathers who have been matured by an intimate relationship with Jesus Christ, teach and instill in their sons love, discipline and sacrifice. They lead by example but are also able to teach their sons about true love, which is to lay down your life for others (your family). *A selfish father will cripple his household!* Then Satan will spoil his household (if there is not a praying wife) because he is the strongman, but he is bound by selfishness, which is the root of all evil.

Mark 3:27 KJVS

*[27] No man can enter into a **strong man's house**, and **spoil his goods**, except he will **first bind the strong man; and then he will spoil his house.***

This is why discipleship is so important! Because being a disciple of Jesus Christ will teach you true love, discipline and sacrifice. Jesus said in John 15 that *greater love has no man than this, that a man lay down his life for his friends.* Jesus was willing to die rather than let Satan spoil his house (which is us)! And we as men must take on that same attitude of love for those entrusted to us. Commitment and faithfulness also go hand in hand with love, discipline and sacrifice. A man who is not faithful to his wife, lacks true love, discipline and the willingness to sacrifice his own desires for the good of his family. Now in balance we know that they're many factors that could lead to infidelity. Some of which could fall heavily on the wife, but in the general sense love, discipline and sacrifice must be growing fruits in a man's life to secure his household. These characteristics of God also help mature the wife and build her up, and also reveal the image of God, manhood and fatherhood to daughters. But we are focusing on sons at the moment. All in all sons will accomplish the Will of mature fathers. And because of this love to accomplish the will of their (mature) fathers, they receive the inheritance. This is the way of God, when a son is matured and is able to accomplish His Will, like Jesus did, He will give him his inheritance!

I was taught by my spiritual father that full inheritance is only given or made accessible at the time of maturity which spiritually is about 20 years. Some may say 20 years? Where did you get that from? Well it took Jesus our Lord 18 years. From the age of 12 where He declared He must be about His Father's business to the age 30 when He was baptized and commissioned. Jesus was perfect and we are not, so it is only fair to think it would take us longer than 18 years to mature. Scripture backs this up in the life of both Joseph and David. It was 20 years from the time of Joseph's dream until he became 2nd in command in Egypt and saved his family from a famine. It was also 20 years from the time David was anointed by Samuel to be king of Israel until the time he took the throne. Maturity takes time and trust must be built in order to be ready to receive your full inheritance from God.

THE REVELATION OF OCCUPATION

Then the devil leaveth him, and, behold, angels came and ministered unto him. (Matthew 4:11)

In this passage of scripture Jesus our Lord had just completed his temptation in the wilderness, after His baptism. His atmosphere was filled with the presence of darkness, because satan had been there to tempt Him. But immediately after the devil had left him, His atmosphere was suddenly filled with the wonderful presence of heaven, as angels came to minister to Him. What can we pull from this scripture? What does the Spirit of God want us to notice?

Here is the revelation: That every atmosphere is occupied, there is no atmosphere or space that is not inhabited by a kingdom. Every place or atmosphere is occupied by either the kingdom of heaven or the kingdom of darkness. So in every space there is a dominant influence. Another way of saying this would be that there is a dominant ministry in every place. What do I mean by dominant ministry?

> *13 But to which of the **angels** said he at any time, Sit on my right hand, until I make thine enemies thy footstool?*
>
> *14 **Are they not all ministering spirits, sent forth to minister** for them who shall be heirs of salvation? (Hebrews 1:13-14)*

Every angel that God ever created is a ministering spirit. This means they have the supernatural ability to influence atmospheres, which in turn influences people. This is why when we go to certain places or enter into certain atmospheres, certain feelings become more dominant, and we feel led to certain actions. What we are feeling is the occupation and ministry influence of that atmosphere.

Every human being on planet earth is constantly being ministered to and influenced by one of two kingdoms (Kingdom of God or the kingdom of darkness). Often when the scripture above is read in church services or Bible studies, it is focused on the angels (ministering spirits) of the Kingdom of God. But we often forget the fallen angels. That these fallen angels of the kingdom of darkness also have this supernatural ability, influence or ministery (1 Timothy 4:1). The simple truth is that every person living will be ministered into heaven or hell. The greater revelation is that we choose what ministry or influence we receive or listen to, and then receive the fruit of that ministry. This is an ancient truth that was lived out in the lives of Adam and Eve. They started out under the influence or ministry of God, but later received the ministry of the devil (serpent) and reaped the fruits (results) of his influence.

For Christians there is a deeper level of darkness and grievous deception that the kingdom of darkness attempts to lord over us. It has to do with the original thirst of satan, which was to rule God's kingdom. Now Jesus told us that the kingdom of heaven is within us, so we house within our bodies the Kingdom of God!

> Neither shall they say, Lo here! or, lo there! for, **behold, the kingdom of God is within you.** (Luke 17:21)

So the devious plans of satan and his kingdom of darkness is to indirectly rule or lord over the kingdom of God by ruling over his temples...us! Because the kingdom of God is within us, the enemy wants to use his ministry or influence to cause us to yield, serve and obey him, all the while carrying the Kingdom of God inside of us. This is some of the hidden twistedness of the mind of satan. Though the kingdom of Heaven in and of itself will never and can never be ruled by satan. Because we are his temple and house His kingdom within us, any victory over us he attributes to himself rulership over the kingdom of God, which is a deception in and of itself.

The kingdom of Heaven is a ministry which we must as followers of Christ receive daily. The sad truth is that many in the body of Christ receive more of the ministry or influence of the kingdom of darkness, than the Kingdom of Light (God). We have to understand that if there is a ministry, then there is a message. Everyday our hearts and minds are bombarded with messages and ministries seeking to influence us, but they only come from two sources (Kingdom of God or the kingdom of darkness). The angels of God are sent to minister righteousness, encouragement, comfort, strength, etc. But the demonic realm comes to minister sin, iniquity, and abomination. These messages that are being sent to us from these two kingdoms are like seeds that go into the ground our hearts and take root, that will eventually sprout up and bear fruit. So what messages we're receiving from the spirit realm, will eventually manifest in the natural realm. Everything that takes place in the natural is a result of a spiritual ministry, whether good or bad. We are ministered into depression, lust, rage, deception, etc by evil spirits. We are also ministered into salvation, joy, peace, faith etc by the angels of God, as well as by the Holy Spirit. But all of this becomes a manifestation of what ministry we have received and what ministry we have rejected.

The Lord Jesus wants us to receive His ministry or influence by whatever means necessary. But He often uses his agents, the angels to bring us messages and to influence us in the right direction. We must learn to discern the influence of the atmospheres we encounter. More importantly we need to team up with the angels of God and minister and influence the atmosphere around us, and allow God through our continuous reception of heavens ministry to create a spiritual climate conducive for His Presence. One major way to do this is praying in tongues! (Also called praying in the Spirit and speaking in unknown tongues in the Bible)

Here is a key and revelation to unlock high and heavenly spiritual climates in your own life and corporately in your local church assemblies: *practice the Presence of God!* How do I practice the Presence of God you may ask? First train your mind always to be God conscious or to think of God always in a relational way. Meaning think of God when you're doing the dishes, walking your dog, driving in your car, while you're at work, it is to co-exist with God. Invite Him into every facet of your life to fellowship with you in whatever you're doing throughout your day. This is how you start to have your mind renewed.

Romans 12:2 KJVS

*[2] And be not conformed to this world: but **be ye transformed by the renewing of your mind**, that ye may prove what is that good, and acceptable, and perfect, will of God.*

To be renewed in your mind literally means to have your mind changed for the better or mind renovation. When you think and meditate on God in a relational way, He gradually becomes more real to you, you experience a greater reality of the presence of God by His Spirit. Doing this magnifies God, it is literally making God greater to you and through you.

Another key to creating a heavenly spiritual climate around you is to study Heaven and what happens in its atmosphere to create what it is tangibly. You do this through the Bible. Heaven is a place of worship in Spirit and in Truth.

John 4:23-24 KJVS

*[23] But the hour cometh, and now is, when the **true worshippers shall worship the Father in spirit and in truth:** for the Father seeketh such to worship him. [24] God is a Spirit: **and they that worship him must worship him in spirit and in truth.***

To worship God in Spirit and in Truth is to join heaven's worship! To understand this we must break the code of what *spirit and truth* is. The Revelation of Spirit and Truth is that it speaks of two Persons of the Godhead. Spirit is speaking of the Holy Spirit and Truth is speaking of Jesus Christ (John 14:6). The Holy Spirit and Jesus are the Worship Leaders in Heaven. They orchestrate the worship that happens around the Father. Here are two examples of this in scripture:

Hebrews 2:11-12 KJVS

*[11] **For both he that sanctifieth and they who are sanctified are all of one:** for which cause he is not ashamed to call them brethren, [12] Saying, **I will declare thy name unto my brethren, in the midst of the church will I sing praise unto thee.***

In this scripture Jesus is Saying that He will sing praise to His Father in the midst or through the church!

Revelation 19:5-7 KJVS

*[5] And **a voice came out of the throne, saying, Praise our God, all ye his servants, and ye that fear him, both small and great**. [6] And I heard as it were **the voice of a great multitude, and as the voice of many waters, and as the voice of mighty thunderings, saying, Alleluia: for the Lord God omnipotent reigneth**. [7] Let us be glad and rejoice, and give honour to him: for the marriage of the Lamb is come, and his wife hath made herself ready.*

This the voice of The Holy Spirit praising and exhorting all of heaven to do so as well. So when the Bible says to worship him in spirit and in truth, it's speaking of worshiping Him in oneness with the Holy Spirit and Jesus! This only comes about through having intimate relationships with them. Jesus is the High Priest (Hebrews 4:14) and the Holy Spirit is His orchestrator. Together they set the atmosphere of Heaven around the Father!

Another key to a heavenly spiritual climate is to give or surrender your senses (sight, hearing, taste, smell, and touch) to God. Allow God to intertwine with and enhance your senses. This is in essence allowing God to permeate your physical body and then the world around you. To do this you must invite Him to saturate your body. You need to physically say these things: "I give you my body and senses" "I surrender my senses to you to sanctify." This is a game changer! When God intermingles with your body you really become a conduit of heaven's atmosphere. When your senses are inclined to God's Heart and His Nature, you're operating as one who dwells in Heaven, being in union with Heaven! This is biblical and mentioned in Romans chapter six.

Romans 6:13-14 KJVS

*[13] Neither yield ye your members as instruments of unrighteousness unto sin: but **yield yourselves unto God, as those that are alive from the dead, and your members as instruments of righteousness unto God**. [14] For sin shall not have dominion over you: for ye are not under the law, but under grace.*

The "members" mentioned in this scripture includes your physical senses. This is actually a great way to overcome sin in your life. Yielding your senses to God delivers you from the carnal man or the nature of the flesh. This process leads to the exponential release of God's Grace in your life! One thing to keep in mind when surrendering and yielding your senses to God, is to know that some of your senses will be more impacted than others, especially at first.

One more key is learning to lean into your love language with God. Know that God knows your love language better than anyone because He created you. So many times He speaks your love language or languages if you have multiple dominant love languages. According to Gary Chapman (author of "*The Five Love Languages*") the five love languages are: words of affirmation, physical touch, quality time, acts of service and receiving gifts.

- **Words of Affirmation:** God will often arouse you spiritually by telling you how he feels about you and things that are great about you as a person. He will lavish you with compliments, and keep in mind God cannot lie. So everything He says about you is absolutely true! (Isaiah 49:15-16)

- **Physical Touch:** God will often manifest His tangible Presence on you and around you. He will make sure you feel His closeness to you, physically. He will let His Power (Anointing) come upon you and use you to lay hands on others and touch their lives. He will even send His angels to be around you, so that you feel their presence, comfort and protection. He will often send anointed men and women into your life to have physical contact with you so that you will feel and experience Him through them. (Luke 4:40)

- **Quality Time:** God will visit you and have extended conversations with you. He will literally come and walk with you like He did with Adam in the garden of Eden. You will have His undivided attention for periods of time. These visitations can often come through dreams and visions, even Him Appearing to you! (Genesis 5:24)

- **Acts of Service:** God will go out of His way to do things for you. Things that you will know without a doubt that it was Him. He will do special things specific to you and to your personal preferences, delights, and desires. He will do things for you just because you asked Him to! (Psalm 68:19)

- **Receiving Gifts:** The Lord will give you gifts from Him, both spiritual and natural gifts. He will give you spiritual gifts that you desire and use you to bless others through those gifts. He will also give you natural gifts (houses, cars, relationships, favors, more time etc) that you desire, even gifts that you didn't ask for just to surprise you! Because He knows you like receiving gifts. (Ephesians 4:8)

A perfect example of differing love languages among believers would be the effect of the Cross. To one whose love language is acts of service just the act of Jesus dying on the cross for them speaks to them very deeply. Whereas a believer who's love language is words of affirmation, hearing the Lord say to them "I did this for you" would speak to them much more than just knowing that he died on the Cross for them. Now to a believer who loves receiving gifts, being able to receive the gift of salvation as a result of Jesus dying for them would minister most to them. The Cross is one act of God, but He ministers it through each individual's love language to have the greatest effect on them.

PERSONAL DEMONIC STRONGHOLDS

Have you ever wondered how demonic spirits come to rule individuals? And eventually communities, cities, and nations? Well the Lord graciously revealed to me through a dream how this process starts. It starts with one individual, being seen by a demon as a target territory. The demonic realm views human beings as territory to conquer and houses to rule over (Matthew 12:44).

This is paramount that we understand how we are *seen* by the enemy. We are cheapened by them and to them, they think of us as nothing more than another notch under their spiritual belt. They see us as nothing more than cheap real estate. So any influence in our lives that comes from the kingdom of darkness is a battle strategy to ultimately *control you!* We must be wise and be on guard against demonic influences that may come in the form of validation that leads to pride, lust, or division in our lives.

I had a dream on December 22, 2018 and there was a man of God named David E. Taylor in this dream. In the dream he was speaking to a young woman and said to her *"Stop letting demons rule you, especially in two areas of your life, this is how they become principalities."* This revelation changed my life in regards to watching over my soul.

This revelation gives great understanding of a method of warfare that the kingdom of darkness uses against us. When a demon or evil spirit wants to rule an individual it's goal is to become dominant in two areas of that person's life or soul. The two areas they dominate establish their reign in your life and makes them a *stronghold* in your life.

Deuteronomy 19:15 KJVS

[15] One witness shall not rise up against a man for any iniquity, or for any sin, in any sin that he sinneth: at the mouth of two witnesses, or at the mouth of three witnesses, shall the matter be established.

As we have just read in the scripture above it takes at least *two witnesses* to establish a matter spiritually before God. A demon ruling one area of your life is *not established,* it must control at least two areas of your life. This is why evil spirits seek to rule in two areas of your life because it establishes them as a stronghold or strongman in your life. The two areas they rule you in serve as *witnesses* to establish their legal right to become a stronghold.

We have to begin to search the weak areas of our life and try to discern any demonic activity that is behind the scenes binding us. If we do not search ourselves and ask the Holy Spirit to reveal any demonic hindrance that may be causing us to fail in different areas of our lives, odds are we will remain blind!

This same principle of establishing rulership is also done in families, cities, and nations! Let's touch on each one of these dimensions of rulership. A demon or evil spirit will work to bind the strongman, this could be the mother or the father depending on the dynamics of the household (single mothers etc). These spirits go after the strongman in a family because they desire what is called the *right of rulership.*

The right of rulership is a spirit's right to rule over in this case a family because it has dominion over the strongman or the head of household. So because they have dominion and authority over the strongman, everyone and everything under the strongman's authority and dominion, it now rules (within the territory of the household). This is how bloodline curses are passed down, these demons have a right to run through the blood or DNA of a family because it runs through the blood and DNA of the strongman. The Bible says that the blood is the *life* of an individual, so the blood is your life in liquid form. This is how the Blood of Jesus saves us, because it's His Life in liquid form covering us!

So whatever areas of dominance it has in your life it's able to attach itself or better put, exercise its authority in that area in your children's lives. This often will be a battle that they will have to overcome themselves.

Now there is a remedy of mercy from God in the procreation process. That if one of the parents has had victory in that area of life, and the other hasn't, it doesn't automatically become a struggle for your offspring. They very well may have no susceptibility or struggle with that area of their lives because of a victorious parent! As we know, DNA's are *combined* from both parents, with both strengths and weaknesses included. This result also initiates the war against the *flesh* that every believer must overcome, to be completely victorious in Christ Jesus!

Satan wants us to find offense in God and in His Word. This is what he did with Eve and he attempts the same with us, and sad to say, in many times he is successful. Jesus made this statement and declaration to the disciples of John in the book of Luke:

Luke 7:23 KJVS

[23] And blessed is he, whosoever shall not be offended in me.

He is talking to Christians, to believers, not unbelievers and the world. The only ones who are *in Christ* are the born again believers. But we allow Satan to stroke our ego and our pride to get us to subconsciously think that we know better or just as much as God. That is a Luciferian mindset that will get you removed from the Body of Christ, ask king Saul! He thought he knew just as much, if not better than God, and the *kingdom* was taken away from him. We do not want the kingdom of Heaven taken away from us, so we must realize that we're *dumb*! That's what sheep are, dumb. They have no direction, so they need a Shepherd to lead them.

Why is it that we think we don't need a Shepherd? That we know what to do? It's pride and arrogance in us that we must kill and remove from our nature. And Satan will boost our foolish ego all the way to our destruction! He will build a city around our *deception* with huge walls entrapping us, so that we cannot get out, but God is our Deliverer!

Deception creates a false world for us to live in, that we believe is real. That is what makes us deceived. God could be revealing the truth to you but you're bound in a world of deception and to you there is no other reality. Even the truth of God seems imaginary, like things could never really be that way, because it's not "reality." This is how our hearts are darkened as the Bible says in Romans.

Romans 1:21 KJVS

[21] Because that, when they knew God, they glorified him not as God, neither were thankful; but became vain in their imaginations, and their foolish heart was darkened.

You see how believers became vain in their imaginations. That word vain in the Greek means morally wicked and idolatrous. Which means to be spiritually twisted in your mind and to have some other *high thoughts* as the idols or gods of your mind instead of the true and living God and Jesus Christ His Son.

This is why we must get the truth of God unto our hearts. Solomon said it this way in Proverbs 7:3 *"...write them on the table on thine heart."*

What is in your heart will control your thought life, and your thoughts produce the words you speak! That's why it says in Proverbs 4:23:

[23] Keep thy heart with all diligence; for out of it are the issues of life.

In other words out of your heart *flows* the words that create the life you live and the world you live in. We ought not to let anything and everything into our hearts because it will enter the spirit of our mind to hinder and deceive us.

Absalom: A Type of The Anti-Christ

There is a very important mystery to glean from the life of Absalom the son of king David. Absalom was raised in the palace and was given the best by his father David. But through a series of disagreements with his fathers decisions, he became rebellious! He ultimately gave in to selfish ambition and allowed pride to rise in his heart. Which led him to plot the overthrow of his father David and to take his throne that God had given him by force. Absalom's life was both an ancient and prophetic (futuristic) picture of Lucifer and the anti-Christ. It was the ancient portrayal of the heart of Lucifer against God the King, who considered him (Lucifer) a son. But in heart he began to let pride and selfish ambition move him to act against God and try to overthrow God's Kingdom and take it for himself. Because he disagreed with God's decision to make mankind with greater glory than himself. God had decided to share His glory and image with mankind and assigned the angels to serve us! So he rebelled against God and was defeated and cast out of the Kingdom of God.

Absalom is also a prophetic picture of the anti-Christ who will rise up against the kingdom of God on earth and make war with his saints. But this attempt to take Jerusalem (The city of God) from The Lord Jesus Christ (God's Appointed King and Ruler), just as Absalom tried to take Jerusalem from his father David (God's appointed king) will be short lived. And just like Absalom, the anti-Christ will be utterly defeated. Then ultimately cast into the lake of fire and brimstone. And the city of God will remain under the dominion of God's Appointed King and Ruler Jesus Christ, just as Jerusalem remained under the dominion of king David (God's appointed king and ruler).

Selfish ambition is a root of rebellion. Do not let selfish ambition or disagreement with those God has placed over you to push you to a path of rebellion. This will not end well for you. The reason it will end badly is because you are rebelling against the direct Authority of God. Anything God decides is for *your best*. Whether you understand His decisions or not is irrelevant, you must trust in His heart for you and others! (Isaiah 55:9)

ONENESS OF MIND: THE HEALING OF THE MIND

We are living in a world that has become vastly aware of the effects of mental illness. I strongly believe this was God's doing of bringing this to light in our day and time. God has much pity and mercy on those who are mentally ill. Mental illness is caused by a lot of different things but they all result in pain, which if not healed turns into mental trauma. Which starts the process of compartmentalization. Which in essence is placing trauma or painful memories in compartments of the brain where you don't have to deal with them. Or even worse, pretend they don't exist or never happened. This starts the process of deception, and living in two different realities. One in which all the trauma is non-existent, which is the lie or deception. The other in which the trauma exists but it is too painful to cope with, sending individuals into cycles of destructive behavior (drugs, violence, suicide etc). Both of these realities are false realities! One reality says trauma (pain) doesn't exist, the other says pain is there and can never be overcome. If these false realities are not dealt with spiritually, you will eventually start to live in two separate realities. Which splits the mind! Mind splitting causes split personalities and schizophrenia. Mind splitting (mental illness/split personalities) is a diabolical strategy of the enemy to make us *untouchable* by God. How does this happen? How do we become untouchable by God? It is because we become double minded. The Bible speaks about this in James 1:6-8.

> *James 1:6-8 KJVS*
>
> *[6] But let him ask in faith, nothing wavering. For he that wavereth is like a wave of the sea driven with the wind and tossed. [7] For let not that man think that he shall receive any thing of the Lord. [8] A double minded man is unstable in all his ways.*

A double minded person is unstable in all of their ways. They're like waves tossed in every direction in their minds, which makes it impossible for them to have faith and keep it. Which then makes it impossible for them to receive anything from The Lord! So if Satan can get you to be double minded, *he can make you untouchable to God.*

This was revealed to me in a vision. In the fall of 2019 I was shown a vision of the human brain and all of a sudden a demon with an axe chopped the brain in half. Then I was told several things, but the solution was **"You must command their minds to be one again."** The healing and deliverance from mind splitting or mental illness is to be commanded by the Authority of Jesus Christ, commanding minds to become *one again!* This is the healing antidote for schizophrenia and split personalities. And depending on how bad the mind is split, it may not happen all at once as others will. But by continuous prayer and declaration for oneness of mind under the anointing there is no case that cannot be healed! The working of The Lord will *surely* take place!

Once the mind is one again the pain or trauma must be dealt with. This may call for deliverance from demonic strongholds and emotional healing. Both of which can be immediate or happen over a process of time.

THE RELATIONSHIP OF HEAVEN

There is an ancient betrayal that happened in eternity that many of us are aware of. It was when Lucifer turned against God and rebelled, taking a third of his angels with him as they were expelled from the Kingdom of God! We must understand that Heaven has been turned on and betrayed by many of its own (the fallen angels). But their existence in Heaven is not wiped from their memories, nor the enlightenment they received while being there. Only it is now corrupted through the darkness that is within them.

Heaven itself trusted those beings and was betrayed. Heaven's heart was broken by betrayal and rebellion, when only goodness was lavished on them continuously. Ungratefulness can manifest in the best of environments, even in perfect environments. So never think because all is well and good, that those close to you cannot betray or turn on you.

This is the ancient lesson in relationships! But we must watch closely the Heart of God in all of this. God still gave Lucifer and the other angels his best for them, knowing they would betray and rebel against Him. He never took away His Love as long as it was received. He only removed His Love when it was rejected by the angelic beings. Even then He never stopped Loving them, he had plans for them in the future and a bright hope for them, but they refused Him.

The wild thing is the mysteries which they learned from God did not depart from them. These were the things the angels who slept with women and bore nephilim (angelic/human hybrids) taught humanity. Forbidden things by The Lord, only to be revealed in His time! When things are revealed before the proper relationship and character is developed in a person, it always results in corruption and tragedy. This is because all wisdom, knowledge, revelation and mystery are not to be known or understood apart from relationship with God. This was the deception of Eve in the garden, she was given knowledge (revelation) apart from her relationship with God and it ultimately separated them (Adam & Eve) from God. This is why Jesus Said in John 16:22 *"I have yet many things to say unto you, but ye cannot bear them now."*

Truth has weight to it, and different truths have different weights. Some are heavier than others and some are lighter. Satan doesn't care if you bear (carry) truth or not, because he's using truth to crush you and I. While God operates completely out of Love and care for us, when revealing and exposing us to things. If you are thirsty for knowledge without God or you are rejecting God while going after knowledge, you will be crushed sooner or later. The Holy Spirit is the Divine Connecter of the dots of God's mysteries in creation! Without Him you are blindly trying to piece together the puzzle of life.

This brings me to my next point: *All light is not good light!* Satan was an angel of glory, but now he is reduced to an angel of (fallen) light. An Angel of light doesn't sound bad to the untrained ear, but that is because most don't understand what all light does. Light always leads to something and initiates a pathway for the spirit man. The Bible says this in 2 Corinthians 11:14-15.

> *2 Corinthians 11:14-15 KJVS*
>
> *[14] And no marvel; for Satan himself is transformed into an angel of light. [15] Therefore it is no great thing if his ministers also be transformed as the ministers of righteousness; whose end shall be according to their works.*

Satan has light in himself but his light does not lead to The Light Jesus Christ! Satan's light takes you on the path to ultimate darkness. This is seen in the new age movement, they begin *enlightened* but end up in *darkness*!

We are lights (Matthew 5:14) but we are lights that lead to The Light Himself (John 8:12). We are pure lights, the devil and his angels are corrupted lights. God's Light causes us to see, but Satan's light blinds us to the truth and causes us to walk in darkness believing we are enlightened. Any light, revelation or knowledge that leads you away from God is corrupted light. A spirit can only give what it has within it (Acts 3:6). If the light in you is corrupted you will only give corrupted light. If it is pure then you will give pure light to others! The only way to be a pure light is to be in relationship with Jesus Christ the Light of the world. All other forms of light are corrupt and are at best gross darkness hidden behind truths.

PRAYER: THE REALITY OF DUAL CITIZENSHIP

Prayer in its simplest form is meant to be communication with God. But the question is where does or where will the communication take place? Is God coming to you or are you going to Him? Or are you both remaining in your prospective locations? These are important aspects of what we call prayer.

In true prayer there is the reality of dual location. Your physical body can be in a certain location on the earth and your spirit can be somewhere else totally different. This is part of the wonder and privilege of being *in* Christ. You can be anywhere that Christ was, is, or is going to be!

Acts 17:28 KJVS

> [28] **For in him we live, and move, and have our being;** *as certain also of your own poets have said, For we are also his offspring.*

This scripture is revealing to us that *in* Him we are alive, and *move* and have our being or identity. Prayer is designed to show us our life in Christ, take us on spiritual journeys, and help reveal our identity to us. The scripture above emphasizes that we are His offspring, which means we have His DNA and are to be like Him. In other words we are to do the same things He does, without limitations! That being said, there is a question we must pose, How do we move in Him? The Bible tells us that there are three primary dimensions in God.

Revelation 1:8 KJVS

[8] I am Alpha and Omega, the beginning and the ending, saith the Lord, **which is, and which was, and which is to come, the Almighty.**

Hebrews 13:8 KJVS

[8] Jesus Christ the same yesterday, and to day, and for ever.

These three dimensions in God are past, present, and future! So because you are in Christ you have access to the past, present and future. Many times these three dimensions are accessed through prayer and waiting on The Lord, as well as by as praise and worship. But now we are focusing on prayer.

You are able to move in Christ into the past, present, or future through prayer. Which means that you can impact all of time with your prayers! Isn't that amazing! Christ the Great Intercessor has given us the same privilege and power that He has through prayer! Prayer is so much more than bowing down on your knees and muttering off words to a Being you don't really expect to hear from. Prayer is a door. You can walk through that door to God and He can walk through that door to you. This is why Jesus said in **"Behold, I stand at the door, and knock: if any man hear my voice, and open the door, I will come in to him, and will sup with him, and he with me."** (Revelation 3:20)

Then He also said in **Matthew 7:7** **"Ask, and it shall be given you; seek, and ye shall find; knock, and it shall be opened unto you."**

So we see in these two scriptures that there is a two way street in the spiritual realm. That we can open our door to God and God can open His door to us. So for the fullness of life in Christ to be experienced there must be willingness by both parties (God and man) to be open with one another. Do you see how if you are shut down or closed off to God or vice versa, that this will hinder movement in the spiritual realm. If a door closes that limits movement, whereas access or the door being opened, it gives greater mobility by being able to go through the door. When doors are open you are able to continue, but if they are shut you're stopped at that door.

I will attempt to explain a great mystery for the sake of understanding prayer. But it's best to use scripture first.

Ephesians 2:6 KJVS

[6] And hath raised us up together, and made us sit together in heavenly places in Christ Jesus:

We are currently in the now, seated in heavenly places in Christ Jesus. But some may say well we're still here on the earth, how are we currently seated in heavenly places? It's called *dual citizenship!* But to understand dual citizenship you have to understand the difference between time and eternity and what it means to be *in Christ*. Here's another scripture to progress in our journey in this mystery.

1 John 4:17 KJVS

[17] Herein is our love made perfect, that we may have boldness in the day of judgment: **because as he is, so are we in this world.**

Here we see that we are presently alive in this world or the natural realm. That we live on this planet called earth and have physical bodies by which we occupy this planet. But this is in the context of *time*. So in *time* we live in the physical world on earth, but in *eternity* we are seated in heavenly places in Christ!

You see, Christ is no longer subject to time. He lives in eternity in Heaven, seated next to His Father. He enters time to visit us and spend time with us but He lives in eternity! Now if we are *in Christ* who lives in eternity, then we also live in eternity, which is the greater realm. So we live on earth in time, but in Heaven in eternity *simultaneously* or at the same time! Jesus spoke of this mystery to Nicodemus.

John 3:13 KJVS

[13] And no man hath ascended up to heaven, but he that came down from heaven, **even the Son of man which is in heaven.**

Jesus is revealing that He came down from Heaven, and was yet currently in Heaven, while He was on earth! Remember 1 John 4:17 that we just read. *As He is, so are we in this world!* We the born again believers live this same life Jesus lived while on earth of dual citizenship!

Now why is this important in the context of prayer? Because you have to understand your abilities and where you can pray from. You can pray in the earth realm to the Heavens or you can pray from Heaven to the earth realm! *You have this liberty and ability!*

Now we must talk about the difference between your *spirit in progression* and your *eternal spirit*. In time our spirit or spirit man is in progression, we are progressively being transformed into our eternal spirit through the process of time! This is the same process Jesus went through when He came to earth. Though He was God in eternity, when He came to earth he became a baby which had to grow and mature into the Eternal Word that He was before time began (John 1:1). This is how God sees us, He sees our eternal spirits that are sitting with Him in heavenly places in Heaven right now! He also sees us in the progression of time and is closely involved in our process into eternity. We have to understand that our eternal spirit has all the understanding that our spirit in progression needs. It is your eternal spirit that joins with the Holy Spirit to make intercession for you according to the will of God. (Romans 8:27)

> *Romans 8:26-27 KJVS*
>
> *[26] Likewise the Spirit also helpeth our infirmities: for we know not what we should pray for as we ought:* **but the Spirit itself maketh intercession for us with groanings which cannot be uttered.** *[27] And he that searcheth the hearts knoweth what is the mind of the Spirit,* **because he maketh intercession for the saints according to the will of God.**
>
> *1 Corinthians 6:17 KJVS*
>
> **[17] But he that is joined unto the Lord is one spirit.**

We see here that our spirit is *one* with God's Spirit. But if our spirit is one with the Lord's Spirit then how is it as the scripture above says, that we *know not* what to pray for as we ought to. Because our spirit man in time or in progress has infirmities, but our eternal spirit does not! It is our eternal spirit in Heaven that joins with the Holy Spirit in unity and prays the Will of God over our lives, helping bring us unto perfection in time! So when you're praying in tongues it is your eternal spirit and The Spirit in *Oneness* in prayer for you! Your eternal spirit knows the language of the Spirit and other languages included in the Kingdom's dialect. Your eternal spirit helps train your spirit in progress to pick up on these languages in time while on earth by the direction of the Holy Spirit. This is how you receive things from God that you cannot articulate, your eternal spirit is housing these treasures in your earthen vessel. Until your spirit in time progresses enough to receive and interpret that dialect from Heaven for others to receive! This is why you may hear Christians say *I understand it but I don't know how to explain it.* What they're really saying in spiritual terms is *I have this treasure in my vessel but I don't know how to handle, interpret, and transfer this treasure because my spirit in progress is not mature enough yet.* This is why the scripture tells us to pray in the Spirit or pray in tongues.

1 Corinthians 14:2 KJVS

*[2] **For he that speaketh in an unknown tongue speaketh not unto men, but unto God:** for no man understandeth him ; **howbeit in the spirit he speaketh mysteries.***

1 Corinthians 14:4 KJVS

*[4] **He that speaketh in an unknown tongue edifieth himself;** but he that prophesieth edifieth the church.*

The first scripture says that when we pray in an unknown tongue we are speaking or having conversations with God. And that in our spirit man we're speaking mysteries. So as we speak to God, our eternal spirit is *speaking mysteries* to our own spirit in progress. This means that our spirit in progress does not always pick up on or receive these mysteries in its understanding. They are *mysteries* that our spirit in progress through growth must receive! That is why the second scripture says that when we speak in an unknown tongue we edify or build up our spirits. Your spirit in progress has to be built up enough to receive or understand the mysteries that have been spoken into it by your eternal spirit, as it received them from God!

Hebrews 9:14 KJVS

*[14] How much more shall the blood of Christ, **who through the eternal Spirit offered himself without spot to God,** purge your conscience from dead works to serve the living God?*

We are in the image of God, and because we are in the image of God our eternal spirit helps us fulfill our destiny, just as the Holy Spirit did in the life of Jesus. The mystery of this is that our spirit and the Holy Spirit are now one (1 Corinthians 6:17). Our eternal spirit works in perfect oneness with *the* Eternal Spirit to lead us into our destiny in God. And when you die or when the rapture takes place we are all transformed or become one into our eternal spirit.

1 Corinthians 15:52-53 KJVS

*[52] In a moment, in the twinkling of an eye, at the last trump: for the trumpet shall sound, and the dead shall be raised incorruptible, and **we shall be changed. [53] For this corruptible must put on incorruption, and this mortal must put on immortality.***

1 John 3:2 KJVS

*[2] Beloved, now are we the sons of God, and it doth not yet appear what we shall be: **but we know that, when he shall appear, we shall be like him;** for we shall see him as he is.*

That phrase *we shall be like Him* is a glorious truth! It means that we will come into our glorified bodies just as He did when He was resurrected from the dead! In other words we will become (transform, change into) our eternal spirit with a glorified body! Our spirits in progress (or spirits in time) will be at a place of maturity to become one with our eternal spirit or eternal identity. This is what Ephesians 4:13 tells us.

Ephesians 4:13 KJVS

*[13] Till we all come in the unity of the faith, and of the knowledge of the Son of God, **unto a perfect man, unto the measure of the stature of the fulness of Christ:***

This is when the fullness of oneness with the Spirit of God is complete! That's what it means to become a *perfect man*, to be fully *one* with God. Just like Jesus is One with The Father. That's the full measure of the stature of Christ, to be totally one with God! This is your destiny with your eternal spirit, as 1 John 3:2 say to *be like Him!* We will be transformed into a *reality* that was already accomplished in eternity! Our spirits just have to go through the process of time to get there.

Time is a believers friend! Time works to help build us up into our eternal spirit or identity. As Romans 8:28 says, *And we know that all things work together for good to them that love God, to them who are the called according to his purpose.* Time is a part of all things. God uses time to push us into our destiny in Him. Within time is what we call *times and seasons.* And as Ecclesiastes 3 tells us every time and season has a purpose, and prayer is designed to reveal and bring us into those purposes.

Did you know that there are many times throughout the Spirit filled believers life when your eternal spirit communicates with your progressional spirit (spirit in time)? (Side note: *If a truth cannot be proven or found in scripture do not build your faith upon it*) When I heard this, I asked The Lord for a scripture to support this revelation that He was giving me and He gave me two! That being said, here are the scriptures to support this mystery:

> *1 Corinthians 14:27-28 KJVS*
>
> [27] *If any man speak in an unknown tongue,* let it be by two, or at the most by three, and that by course; and let one interpret. [28] But if there be no interpreter, let him keep silence in the church; *and let him speak to himself,* and to God.
>
> *Psalm 42:11 KJVS*
>
> [11] *Why art thou cast down, O my soul? and why art thou disquieted within me?* hope thou in God: for I shall yet praise him, who is the health of my countenance, and my God.

Here we see in these two scriptures eternal spirit and progressional spirit (spirit in time) communication! In 1 Corinthians the scripture instructs one to speak to *himself* and to God. This goes back to 1 Corinthians 6:17 that says he that is joined to The Lord is one spirit. So when you speak in an unknown tongue you are not only speaking to God but to your eternal spirit that is in God or as the scripture says, one with God. But your communication with your eternal spirit is a mystery, meaning it is not conceivable by the natural mind. It must be interpreted or understood spiritually. What your eternal spirit communicates to you will always edify you (build you up).

Sometimes we think that we're hearing from the Holy Spirit (and in a sense you are) but you're actually hearing from your eternal spirit. I'll give you an example: when a man or woman of God is ministering or speaking by the inspiration of the Holy Spirit, that person is speaking but it's actually the Holy Spirit speaking through them. So I may be looking at Sam speaking but it's also the Holy Spirit speaking through Sam. This is an example of your spirit being one with The Lord. You as a person are speaking but it's actually the Holy Spirit speaking through you. This is what happens when your eternal spirit who is one with The Lord is speaking or communicating to you. Your eternal spirit always speaks from oneness with The Lord!

This is what was being manifested in Psalm 42:11! King David's eternal spirit in Heaven with God was speaking to his soul in time on earth. His eternal spirit was questioning his soul about its discouragement and encouraging his soul at that present time to *hope in God!* That is amazing and our eternal spirit has the capacity to do the same and even greater because we are in the New Covenant!

Nehemiah 2 "The Gates of Prayer"

Nehemiah 2:13-14 KJVS

*[13] And I went out by night by the **gate of the valley**, even before **the dragon well**, and to the **dung port**, and **viewed the walls of Jerusalem**, which were broken down, and the gates thereof were consumed with fire. [14] Then I went on to the **gate of the fountain**, and to **the king's pool:** but there was no place for the beast that was under me to pass.*

These two verses are a revealed mystery of a process in prayer. Whether we realize it or not we go through spiritual gates in prayer, having this wisdom and understanding will rid many of our frustrations in prayer. There are so many Christians who honestly dread and avoid prayer because they don't understand the spiritual process or journey that they're embarking upon. If you could track or understand your prayer journey, you would be relieved of your frustration. You would also acquire hope and your faith would increase by the realization of progress in your prayer journey.

We first have to understand that there are levels and depths in prayer and that this process of prayer is not always *the process* of prayer depending on where your spirit is with GOD. This process of prayer is for those entering into the depths of prayer for the first time and to give understanding to those believers who are seasoned in prayer. The reality is that many seasoned saints or Christians as we say, experience a great deal of frustration and discouragement in prayer. This mystery in prayer is a *message of hope, encouragement, and understanding!* It will ignite you to press into your prayer journey because you know there is a path and destination. I'm excited to reveal these mysteries in prayer, lets examine the scriptures!

Nehemiah 2:13-14 KJVS

*[13] And I went out by night by the **gate of the valley**, even before **the dragon well**, and to the **dung port**, and viewed the **walls of Jerusalem, which were broken down**, and **the gates thereof were consumed with fire**. [14] Then I went on to the **gate of the fountain**, and to the **king's pool**: but there was **no place for the beast that was under me to pass**.*

The first gate we come to in prayer is the *gate of the valley*. The gate of the valley is the entrance into prayer through humility or humbling yourself. A valley is a low place and lowliness speaks of humility. This is also the beginning of death to self or crucifying our flesh in prayer.

1 Peter 5:6 KJVS

*[6] **Humble yourselves** therefore under the mighty hand of God, that he may exalt you in due time:*

So by lowering ourselves we are prophesying our future elevation or exaltation by God. This is paramount in prayer if we're going to finish the journey that prayer is designed to take us on. Enter into the *gate of the valley*, start low, be humble and let God lift you up in prayer!

Once we enter into the *gate of the valley*, which is the gate of humility, you soon enter into the **dragon well**. The dragon well can actually be translated as the *serpent pool*. This is the place in prayer where you encounter all of the stray thoughts, distractions, accusations of satan etc. Those things are all serpents swimming around or circulating in our minds, but usually aren't manifest until we go into prayer.

We must kill all of the serpents in the well of our mind if we're going to move on in prayer. These are usually killed through *repentance* and *meditating or rehearsing the Word of God* in prayer. This is how Jesus overcame satan in the wilderness. He didn't need to repent as we do, being imperfect, but

He rehearsed the Word in His heart and mind and spoke the Word to overcome satan, who is called the serpent. We should follow this pattern also, as Christ is our example (1 Peter 2:21). This also may take *time* in prayer, that is why it is important not to be in a rush when you pray but to learn to *wait* on The Lord. *Sadly this is where many stop or give up in prayer.*

Next in prayer we come to what is called the **dung port.** This is the gate where God by His Spirit begins to deal with our *mess or filth.* He starts to address certain issues or ways about us that are not like Him, and reveal them to us. This is the *place of acknowledgement.* This is where we start to get uncomfortable and even defensive. Our fallen human nature is to justify our wrongs instead of humbling ourselves and confessing, and we often do this with God in prayer. But we must remember that we've entered through the gate of the valley, which is the gate of humility and you must remain humble to get to the promised land in prayer!

Matthew 5:3 KJVS

*[3] Blessed are the **poor in spirit**: for theirs is the **kingdom of heaven.***

If you are going to gain entrance into the Kingdom of Heaven, which is the believers promised land, you must remain humble or poor in spirit. Do not get defensive when God brings us your shortcomings or the unsanctified areas of your life. He's only doing it to strengthen and heal you, so that you become better! This process also makes you more *like Him* and brings you closer to Him.

Then we come to the **walls of Jerusalem, which were broken down.** Which represents the walls that we place around our hearts, between us and God, that He breaks down. This is the place of *transparency*, where we must put our guard down and be completely *broken* as the scripture says, before The Lord. We must become *broken spirits* before God, totally open and vulnerable with Him, this is where *trust* in the Lord is birthed and built up in our relationship with God.

Psalm 34:18 KJVS

*[18] The Lord is nigh unto them that are of a **broken heart; and saveth such as be of a contrite spirit.***

Psalm 51:17 KJVS

*[17] The sacrifices of God are a **broken spirit**: a broken and a contrite heart, O God, thou wilt not despise.*

After this we come to a place where **the gates thereof were consumed with fire.** This is the purifying process in prayer, some call it *purging.* This is after the acknowledgment and brokenness, that God begins to purify your soul. Purging you from impurities through prayer. This is also God's cleansing process in prayer, preparing us for Himself. If we allow God to purify us through prayer we get the reward of intimacy with Him in a deeper way!

James 4:8 KJVS

*[8] Draw nigh to God, and he will draw nigh to you. Cleanse your hands, ye sinners; and **purify your hearts,** ye double minded.*

This brings us spiritually to the **gate of the fountain!** This is the place where God begins to pour into us and feed our thirsty souls with the living waters of Heaven. After we have allowed Him to deal with us and purify us.

Matthew 5:6 KJVS

*[6] Blessed are they which do hunger and thirst after righteousness: for **they shall be filled.***

There is a revelation in this scripture that reveals and confirms this process in prayer. That if you're still hungry and thirsty *after righteousness,* meaning after you've allowed Him to cleanse you and make you right before him in prayer, ***then you will be filled!*** We must go through the process of righteousness in prayer. Which is being convicted, broken, transparent, acknowledging, and being purged. All these things lead to and through the *gate of the fountain!* This is where we are satisfied by The Lord, but we must go on in prayer and *satisfy Him!*

I also must make note that this process can happen in one prayer session or through many prayer sessions. For example you could go through this whole process in one hour of prayer or you could spend a month working through each phase of prayer. *There is no specific timeline, only the leading of The Spirit!*

Then finally we come to the **king's pool.** This is where The Lord becomes open and transparent with us! Where he begins to *reveal Himself* in a special and intimate way. Only the king's bride and his children were allowed in the *king's pool*, and we are *both* his children and his bride. It is a place reserved for those who are closest to the king! For those who have gone through the process in prayer to be brought before the king in his personal and intimate pool, which represents the *secret place!* The place of His dwelling where those who have been prepared are personally invited to come. This is a very *sacred place* with The Lord.

It is interesting how the scripture is summed up saying *"but there was no place for the beast that was under me to pass."* This symbolizes a separation from the flesh (beast) and being released into the Spirit! This reveals that only the one who has gone through this process in prayer can enter the king's pool. It symbolized a man riding on a horse or donkey through this process, which would represent *prayer*. We're riding on this journey of prayer through every other gate and process *except* to get into the king's pool. The reason is because now it is not merely *prayer* anymore, it is *intimacy with God!* This is where you get to know Who The Lord is as a Person and not just as your God. You get to know Him as your Lover and not just as your Lord and King. As I said before, it is a secret place with Him that is by personal invitation only. This is a process in prayer that if you're faithful and diligent, will release eternal benefits. The greatest benefit being knowing The Lord intimately Face to face!

THE PRAYER LADDER

Genesis 28:12 KJVS

[12] And he dreamed, and behold a ladder set up on the earth, and the top of it reached to heaven: and behold the angels of God ascending and descending on it.

We see through this scripture that there is a ladder from Heaven to earth and the angels of God ascend and descend on this ladder. This ladder is a spiritual ladder, which means it's not a normal ladder but it's supernatural! God wants and desires us to climb this supernatural ladder.

I was given a vision in prayer of this ladder by The Spirit of God. In this vision the Lord Jesus was standing by this ladder and He stretched out His Hands toward the ladder. In each space in the ladder where our feet and hands would normally go was a portal or gate that we have access to when we reach that level on the ladder.

There is a gate at each level of the ladder. At each gate there are also angels as guardians of the gates. This is part of how you encounter angels ascending and descending the great ladder. These angels allow you access into the different gates of the ladder. The gate that is the most appealing to you is the revelation of your spirit (it's condition or state of being).

Many never go past the gates of petition. The *gates of petition* are the lowest gates on the ladder of God. Though they do ascend higher according to our faith and the greatness of the petition. The reason many never ascend past the gates of petition is that their desire to *be known* is greater than their to *know*.

1 Corinthians 13:12 KJVS

[12] For now we see through a glass, darkly; but then face to face: now I know in part; but then **shall I know even as also I am known.**

We must come to the conclusion that we are *known* of God or we will only *know* God on certain levels. To *know* is the highest petition in prayer and will give you access to any gate. That is part of how you will *know* even as you are *known,* as the scripture above says.

Our highest petitions are to God The Father and Jesus Christ His Son. There is nothing more important than that. Knowing Them is eternal life!

John 17:3 KJVS

[3] And this is life eternal, that they might know thee the only true God, and Jesus Christ, *whom thou hast sent.*

Our hearts desire ought to be to know The Lord Jesus Christ intimately. He is the manifestation of God in the flesh and the express image of His Person or Personality. He is the Mediator between God and man and our access to God.

2 Peter 3:18 KJVS

[18] But grow in grace, and **in the knowledge of our Lord and Saviour Jesus Christ.** *To him be glory both now and for ever. Amen.*

Philippians 3:8,10 KJVS

[8] Yea doubtless, and I count all things but loss **for the excellency of the knowledge of Christ Jesus my Lord:** *for whom I have suffered the loss of all things, and do count them but dung,* **that I may win Christ, [10] That I may know him,** *and the power of his resurrection, and the fellowship of his sufferings, being made conformable unto his death;*

Knowing Christ intimately is the prerequisite for knowing The Father intimately. You must first love and honor the Son to receive and be prepared to love and honor The Father the way you are supposed to. It is Jesus Who gives us access to The Father and ultimately releases us to Him to be trained by Him at the appointed time.

Luke 10:22 KJV

*[22] All things are delivered to me of my Father: and no man knoweth who the Son is, but the Father; and who the Father is, but the Son, **and he to whom the Son will reveal him.***

Galatians 4:2 KJV

*[2] But is under tutors and governors **until the time appointed of the father.***

There is a process of relationship that has to be developed with Jesus in order for Him to begin revealing the Father to you. Jesus Said that He is The Door (Access Point). But what is He the Door to? The answer is The Father! Jesus did not die to restore and reconcile man to Himself but to The Father. That is the mystery of St. John 15:13!

John 15:13 KJV

*[13] **Greater love** hath no man than this, **that a man lay down his life for his friends.***

Jesus was ultimately laying His Life down for His Best Friend, His Father! That is the Greatest Love of all the Love Relationship between Jesus and His Father. His Father desired Him to be the Sacrifice for all mankind and the Mediator who would bring all men back to Himself. Yes Jesus laid down His Life for us, but He was ultimately doing it to restore all of mankind to God. He was not just dying to bring us to God, but to bring God to us! Which is the greatest realm of relationship that mankind can have. The greatest relationship that humanity can have is not with Jesus, but with The Father! This is the relationship that Jesus prizes more than anything, and His desire and prayer is that we be a part of it.

John 17:21-23 KJVS

*[21] That they all may be one; as thou, Father, art in me, and I in thee, **that they also may be one in us:** that the world may*

believe that thou hast sent me. [22] ***And the glory which thou gavest me I have given them; that they may be one, even as we are one:*** *[23] I in them, and thou in me, that they may be made perfect in one; and that the world may know that thou hast sent me, and hast loved them, as thou hast loved me.*

When this relationship is built with The Father our prayer life will change drastically! Because once we finish our process through Jesus of being prepared for The Father Personally. We will develop our own personal intimacy with Him, not just through Jesus as our Mediator. Jesus Said this:

John 16:23,26-27 KJVS

[23] ***And in that day ye shall ask me nothing.*** *Verily, verily, I say unto you,* ***Whatsoever ye shall ask the Father*** *in my name,* ***he will give it you.*** *[26] At that day ye shall ask in my name:* ***and I say not unto you, that I will pray the Father for you:*** *[27]* ***For the Father himself loveth you,*** *because ye have loved me, and have believed that I came out from God.*

PRAYING IN TONGUES, MYSTERIES, & ANGELS

Praying in tongues has become a worldwide phenomenon in the Body of Christ at large. Over the past few decades much of the church regardless of denomination has accepted this manifestation of the Spirit of God. But what most don't understand is that praying in tongues is many times, the longest conversations that we have with God. It is because of one simple truth: *God speaks Mystery!*

> *1 Corinthians 14:2 KJVS*
>
> *[2] For he that speaketh in an unknown tongue speaketh not unto men, **but unto God**: for no man understandeth him ; **howbeit in the spirit he speaketh mysteries.***

Mystery is the language of God. Just like we in America speak English, God speaks mystery. This is what Adam and God spoke on their daily walks together. This is what Enoch *who walked with God* learned to speak fluently. As most people know, long walks together are primarily for lovers and close friends. As we gradually grow in our relationship with God, we will learn His language and become more accustomed to digesting His content with understanding. Which turns into longer conversations!

Praying in tongues actually builds up our spirit to be able to receive and perceive God (**1 Corinthians 14:4**). It's building up our spirit to take in or receive larger portions of God (**Psalm 119:57**). It's just like here on earth as we grow our appetite and ability to consume more food increases. As babes we drink milk and it's the same spiritually (**Hebrew 5:13/1 Peter 2:2).** But God does not intend for us to stay there but to grow and mature and begin to eat the meat of the Word. Because God likes to talk mystery, His Words are like strong meat as the Word Says in **Hebrews 5:14.**

What happens when we continually pray in the Spirit (in tongues) we are becoming more and more fluent in the language of God. And the spirit of our mind takes over our natural brain and the breaking down or decoding of the mysteries of God starts to register with us in the natural realm. But you must be intentional about understanding the unknown tongue or the language of mysteries. It is only an unknown tongue to us, not to God or Heaven. What I mean by being intentional is it must be a sincere desire, not a casual desire. You must pursue this and seek to know it!

1 Corinthians 14:13-14 KJVS

*[13] Wherefore **let him that speaketh in an unknown tongue pray that he may interpret.** [14] For if I pray in an unknown tongue, my spirit prayeth, but my understanding is unfruitful.*

Now how do you know when you're starting to understand (interpret) the language of mysteries or unknown tongues? As previously stated, unknown tongues are the language of God. So how do you know that you're beginning to understand the language of God? Many times it starts with the senses. If you're praying in the Spirit and you start to see images of certain people or places, your spiritual receptors are now picking up God's signal and translating it through your natural mind or brain. He's using the sense of sight. If you're praying in tongues and you start to hear words, maybe even just one word, your understanding is now coming through the sense of hearing. Many times they are words we think we know but there is a deeper meaning to them that God wants to bring out. He's doing this in order to help us and/or others. These are often answers to prayers we prayed in the Spirit. Sometimes they are words we don't know and we have to look up the meaning or find those words in the Bible and the context around which they were used. They may be showing us where we are with God or qualities we need to develop in our lives.

Then sometimes while praying in the Spirit you will begin to feel things or have knowledge about certain things. This is God speaking to you through the sense of spiritual touch. You're feeling what God is saying, not necessarily hearing or seeing it. And that feeling or knowing directs you in prayer in the language of our understanding (native language). But you do not have to pray in the language of your understanding once direction is given to your natural mind in prayer. You can continue praying in the Spirit for that person by keeping them in your mind or before your face in your imagination. There is a great scripture that highlights this:

Ephesians 3:20 KJVS

[20] Now unto him that is able to do exceeding abundantly above all that we ask or think, according to the power that worketh in us,

The Scripture shows us that God not only works through what we ask but what we *think* or our *thoughts!* But He does this through us working with the Holy Spirit in prayer. So you are just as effective thinking of someone in prayer as you are praying about them out of your mouth, when praying in the Spirit!

One key for effectiveness in prayer for others using the power of thought is you must use your sanctified imagination! You must see them through initiating a vision of the good you want to see for them. Also by partnering with the Holy Spirit to see His vision for them and pray into what He shows you. This practice is a part of what is mentioned in Romans 12:21:

Romans 12:21 KJV

[21] Be not overcome of evil, but overcome evil with good.

Most times when you're praying for someone it is because there is some sort of obstacle or hindrance in their lives. By using your sanctified imagination you get the privilege and opportunity to overcome the evil that is against them with the good of your thoughts (which is the language of Heaven), and God is able to work through your thoughts to bring about change and breakthrough in their lives. This same principle applies for you personally as well. Think good about yourself and envision good for yourself because that's what God and all of Heaven is doing!

Proverbs 23:7 KJVS

[7] For as he thinketh in his heart, so is he...

There is another way of prayer that we must also mention and it is spoken of in 1 Corinthians 14:15.

1 Corinthians 14:15 KJV

[15] What is it then? I will pray with the spirit, and I will pray with the understanding also: I will sing with the spirit, and I will sing with the understanding also.

That way is to pray *with* the Spirit. To pray with the Spirit is to pray Spirit inspired or led prayers. This is different from praying from your own priorities or concerns. This is a type of prayer that is the manifestation of the Holy Spirit's agenda, not ours. When we pray *with* the Spirit it is different from praying *in* the Spirit in that we are not praying in tongues. Generally when we pray with the Spirit we are praying in our native language and with natural understanding of what is being said. In this case we must yield our agendas and priorities in prayer to the Holy Spirit and take on His Will in prayer. This is not easy for the common believer, because we are used to praying our own agendas and priorities. So it is hard for us at first to relinquish and surrender those things, and pick up the Will of the Spirit in prayer. This is a selfless act of love and should be done consistently, so that it becomes common in our prayer lives.

One way to pray *with* the Spirit is through dreams and visions. We must take what The Holy Spirit is revealing to us in dreams as prayer points or focus points in prayer. He will show us through dreams things we need to pray for and things He is emphasizing. He will also give us visions and instruct us what to pray for. Some of us may receive visionary pictures that are giving us insight into what to pray for. Some may see flashes of images in your mind, these are focal points that the Spirit is emphasizing. And if we lean into them will lead us into praying with The Spirit!

Another way we pray with the Spirit is through the weighty spirit of intercession. When this happens there is a burden of prayer that comes on an individual. You may not even know what you're burdened about but you know it's time to pray! Many times these prayer burdens from The Lord will cause you to weep and mourn. You may not even speak or use words but just weep and cry out to The Lord beyond the point of words. This type of prayer is spoken of in Romans 8:26.

Romans 8:26 KJVS

[26] Likewise the Spirit also helpeth our infirmities: for we know not what we should pray for as we ought: but the Spirit itself maketh intercession for us with groanings which cannot be uttered.

There is another type of prayer or praying in tongues, called the tongues of angels referenced in 1 Corinthians 13:1.

1 Corinthians 13:1 KJVS

[1] Though I speak with the tongues of men and of angels...

To be clear the Bible speaks of three main types of tongues. Those three are: the tongues of men, angels and the unknown tongue. We've discussed the unknown tongue which is the language of communication between God and our spirit (1 Corinthians 14:2). The tongues of men are different dialects spoken supernaturally by men or women who have no knowledge of that dialect to deliver a message from God. This is often the type of tongues that is being spoken when the gifts of diversity of tongues and interpretation of tongues are in manifestation. The tongues of men are often used by God when someone is being baptized in the Holy Spirit and speaking in tongues. It was termed as *other tongues* in Act 2:4. In other words speaking supernaturally in a tongue *other* than what you naturally speak. This is shown in Acts 2:6-8 as well.

Acts 2:6-8 KJVS

[6] Now when this was noised abroad, the multitude came together, and were confounded, because that every man heard them speak in his own language. [7] And they were all amazed and marvelled, saying one to another, Behold, are not all these which speak Galilaeans? [8] And how hear we every man in our own tongue, wherein we were born?

Then there are the tongues of angels. This is very useful and vital to the believer, though many never really think about it. The tongues of angels are the spiritual language by which the angels communicate. God in His Goodness and Sovereignty has chosen to give us this ability in order to accomplish His Will on earth. When we speak in the tongues of angels in prayer, we are communicating to them the Will of God and their assignments. In essence we are giving the angels instructions to follow in order to accomplish the Will of God on the earth. Sometimes when you're speaking in tongues of angels you will see visions of angels doing certain things and going to certain places. It is because you're being shown by The Spirit what you're communicating to the angels to do and get done. He (Holy Spirit) is showing you your effectiveness in the spiritual realm!

Psalm 103:20 KJVS

*[20] Bless the Lord, ye his angels, that excel in strength, that do his commandments, **hearkening unto the voice of his word.***

The Scripture states that the angels of God hearken to the voice of His Word. When we as the temples of the Holy Spirit pray in the tongues of angels, we become the voice of His Word! We become the vessel through which He is speaking to the angels and giving them their commandments. Praying in the tongues of angels activates a high level of angelic activity in your life and to those around you!

On the flip side there are also demonic tongues. These are the supernatural tongues or language of demons (evil spirits). Some have experienced these kinds of tongues when administering deliverance to others or from people who are in the occult trying to wage warfare against believers and the atmosphere of Heaven. If you have just adequate spiritual discernment, you will discern these tongues because of the presence or atmosphere they release. These tongues release the atmosphere of demons and demonic activity, just as the tongues of angels release the atmosphere of Heaven and angelic activity. There are literal battles that are won and lost on the basis of tongues from the angelic realms. The angels of God are His warriors and agents to help accomplish His Will on earth. So we can help and empower them by praying in tongues and thereby creating an atmosphere conducive for Heavenly dominion in the earth!

LOVE OR MANIPULATION

This message alone is and will be a deliverance to many in the Body of Christ that read it. Many of us are operating in and using witchcraft on those we are closest to and don't even know it. The scripture says it like this:

2 Corinthians 2:11 KJVS

[11] Lest Satan should get an advantage of us: for we are not ignorant of his devices.

Satan can take advantage or get an advantage over us if we are ignorant of his devices or strategies. One of the greatest and most subtle ways he does this is through *manipulation*. I was shown this by The Lord in a vision, where He revealed to me that I was operating in the power of witchcraft, which was manipulation. I didn't recognize the darkness that was in my heart until the Spirit shined His light on my condition.

What I was doing was manipulating my wife to get her to do what I wanted her to do, instead of allowing her the choice to do those things out of love for me, like The Lord does to us! I was subtly saying the right things or saying little things to steer her in the direction I wanted her to go. I would do things because I knew it would get a certain reaction or response out of her, based on what I desired. That is witchcraft! To deceive the mind of another by creating a reality that stems from darkness, selfishness and pride.

Love has the other person's best interest at heart, *not your own*. Pure love causes us to become servants of one another, not manipulators. The question is: *Is your love pure or tainted with selfish desires, pride and ambition?* If it is, Satan is using you and taking advantage of you and you don't even know it. See, our hearts are desperately wicked, the Bible says, so Satan uses the evil desperations of our hearts to lure us away from pure love! If the motive for your actions is not pure it's defiled...think about that! If I buy my wife flowers because I want her to give me sexual pleasure, instead of purely demonstrating my love for her, I'm trying to manipulate her into fulfilling my selfish desire. Love seeks to meet needs but manipulation seeks how to fulfill its own needs. It's pride and selfishness, it is also a device of Satan to use against us and to keep us impure in our hearts. Watch your motives, they will tell you whether you're being led by the Spirit or by the flesh. When you can still love unconditionally even when your needs aren't being met, then your heart is right and operating out of pure love! But if you're upset, spiteful, bitter, and vengeful when your needs aren't met but someone else's is, your heart is a breeding ground for a spirit of manipulation. Be careful of this trap! It will be easier now because you are no longer ignorant of this device of Satan and will be able to spot it in yourself and others as well, praise God!

This brings me to the next revelation, which I was given in a dream. In this dream I was shown a heavenly book, it was a beautiful crimson red with gold letters on it. The title of the book was *"Lust in Marriage."* When I finished reading the title of the book, The Lord Jesus spoke to me and Said ***"You should talk about this."***

At that time I didn't know what to say about it. But soon after the Holy Spirit began to give me revelation about this subject. He began to illuminate my mind to the different ways that we lust in marriage and how many times we allow lust to rule instead of love.

The Spirit began to show me scenarios of how a husband may sexually desire his wife but she is not in the mood so to speak. He revealed to me if he changes how he treats her because of this, he's being ruled by lust and not love. Because he's placing her physical body as the priority and not her heart or her as a person. So if the physical body is not given to him, he then begins to treat her in a negative way or hurtful way. At the very least, in a careless way.

This revelation struck a chord with me because I knew I had been guilty of this. And immediately I had to start making internal adjustments to make sure I'm not allowing lust to rule me in my marriage. But more so making adjustments to make sure *love is ruling* in my marriage. Lust is rooted in selfishness and will be fulfilled if there is no self control, which is a fruit of The Spirit we must grow and progress in. Love is selfless, it is about putting others first. Love and lust are complete opposites and their intentions are opposing. These intentions will eventually manifest.

One thing about the human spirit is that it can't feel lust. In a way I believe that it doesn't feel anything else, except for love! We know and can physically feel when someone desires us in a lustful way. Depending on whether we feel the same or not, many times will determine our response to them. Much of the sex that goes on in the world on a daily basis is a mutual response to lust. So we form sex lives or sexual patterns based off of lust, which is very short sighted. Lust pulls on the body, while love on the other hand pulls on the heart. So if we are not used to being pulled or exercised by love, then our *emotional muscle memory* has been exercised by lust. Many of our relationships ended badly prior to marriage or even in marriage because lust was the driver not love. And many believers are unknowingly bringing this (lust driven desire) into marriage, instead of love driven desires.

Now we have to clarify that lust is *not* just sexual, but it is a strong carnal desire not rooted in love. That desire could be for control, money, notoriety etc. Lust can branch off many different ways but so can love. So many Christians have to be delivered from lust driven marriages. One key sign that you're operating in a lust driven marriage is that when your lust is not fulfilled, there is the manifestation of anger, rage, resentment, violence, slander, and the love that you do have in your marriage you quickly take back. This shows that love is not driving your marriage but lust is driving your marriage. It doesn't mean that there is no love there, but it will always be affected by the fulfillment or lack thereof of your lusts. This reveals that your love is not unconditional but conditional, and that is not the love of Christ!

The Bible Says that God is Love (1 John 4:8+16). The Bible also says that

God is faithful (Deuteronomy 7:9). So God's Nature is Love and He is consistent (faithful) in His Nature. So true love if it is driving or ruling in your marriage, is consistent, even if certain desires are not being met. Now that does not mean that it is easy by any means, but because love is the driving force of your marriage it remains consistent. You are actually empowered by God to love supernaturally in an unconditional way. God's Love in you breeds selflessness in the heart and trains your heart to put the other person (your spouse) first. Now in balance, spouses should *not be holding out* on each other. This is not the Will of GOD nor is it healthy for your marriage. But for the times when it does happen, we are to be governed by love!

1 John 4:16 KJVS

*[16] And we have known and believed the love that God hath to us. **God is love; and he that dwelleth in love dwelleth in God, and God in him.***

We all must be watchful and see if lust is ruling or driving our marriages. Or is love the ruling and abiding force in our marriages. This in many cases will determine our success or lack thereof in marriage.

TO KNOW HIM & TO ABIDE IN HIM

Acts 17:28 KJVS

*[28] **For in him we live, and move, and have our being;** as certain also of your own poets have said, For we are also his offspring.*

What I've learned over the past couple of years on my walk with The Lord, is that there is a vast difference between knowing Him and abiding in Him. There have been two experiences with The Lord that really drove this point home with me and opened my eyes to this spiritual truth. The first was a dream that I received in 2018 in which there was a man dressed in a gray suit who was wandering around in the dark. Then a small light appeared in the distance before the man and he began walking toward the light. I knew and understood by the Spirit in this dream that this man represented the church. The man (church) followed this light out of the darkness into the light of this present time. Then all of a sudden Lord Jesus appeared and the man was standing before the Lord and the Lord was smiling. But what I noticed about the Lord (having seen Him before in dreams and visions) was that He looked a little malnourished. This stood out to me and I would soon find out why. As the man was standing before the Lord Jesus, the Lord spoke these words to him, ***"You rejoiced in coming out of the darkness, but you've not yet learned to abide in the Light."*** This statement struck me and I took it personally, as I should have. But this message was not to me alone but is also for the church at large. Jesus was revealing that we as the church, the body of Christ, have in the past decades rejoiced in coming out of the darkness (the world, sin, wickedness) but we've not yet learned to abide in Him: The Light! There was an overwhelming sense that we (the church) had made them almost the same. That *coming out of darkness* and *abiding in the light* were combined as one spiritual experience to us, but this is not true!

Then in the dream Jesus told the man to come *into Him* and the man sort of brashly tried to enter into the Lord and he went right through him. Then the Lord had him try again and the second time he was more humble and meek and graciously walked into the Lord Jesus and the man was gone. The only one who remained was the Lord Jesus! But as the man entered the Lord, it was if the Lord was breathing him in or inhaling him into His Body with such pleasure and satisfaction! Then the Holy Spirit began to reveal to me why Jesus was malnourished in the dream. *It was because much of the church is not abiding IN HIM!* That He would be more full and satisfied if His people were abiding in Him! We are His satisfaction. We cause Him to suffer starvation when we don't abide in Him. Jesus said in St. John 4:32 *"But he said unto them, I have **meat to eat that ye know not of**."* Jesus' meat was to do the Will of The Father and part of the Will of The Father is for us to abide in Jesus (St. John 15:4). And in Him we will bear much fruit and He eats the Fruit of The Spirit. Its nourishment for Him for us to dwell in Him and bear much fruit (St. John 15:5).

The second experience came to me in early 2019 while in the shower. I was just thinking about the things of the Lord and different events that had been taking place and pondering God's heart concerning those things. As I was doing this the Lord Jesus spoke these words to me in my spirit, ***"Paige, I need you to learn to abide in Me."*** This immediately gave me the revelation and enlightenment that I was not abiding in Him. This is when it really began to sink into my spirit the vast difference between *knowing Him* and *abiding in Him.* You see, there are times when we seek the Lord and He reveals Himself to us. There are moments when we spend time with the Lord and fellowship with Him and He gives us insight into His Heart. And as a result of those things we get to know Jesus better, but that does not mean we are *like Him.* Whatever we see in The Lord or He reveals to us about Himself, we are to be transformed into that same image (2 Corinthians 3:18). We are to become what we see in Him and what is revealed to us about Him. To be in Him is to yield our total being to Him, His Nature, His Movements.

The sad truth is that many of us know Him more than we abide in Him, and this is grievous to the Lord. He longs for us to dwell in Him, to satisfy His desire to be with us and one with us. One of the biggest mistakes many well meaning Christians make is going on lifelong quests to know more about Him, while failing to dwell in Him by becoming what they know about Him. It requires a deeper fellowship and surrender to dwell in Him, where the whole quest is to become *one with Him* in His heart and nature.

John 17:21 KJVS

*[21] That they all may be one; as thou, Father, art in me, and I in thee, **that they also may be one in us:** that the world may believe that thou hast sent me.*

The Mystery & Revelation of Gifts

James 1:17 KJVS

[17] Every good gift and every perfect gift is from above, and cometh down from the Father of lights, with whom is no variableness, neither shadow of turning.

Every spiritual gift is given from God, Who is Light. They literally come out of Him and are sent down to earth to be received by mankind. If God is light and gifts come out of him to us, then gifts themselves are also *light.* They are portions of light from God given to man by which to know, reveal and glorify God.

Now because gifts come down or descend, they have the *spirit of humility* on them. For anything in a high place to come down to a lower place and dwell takes humility. This is also what Jesus did, He humbled himself and came down to earth to save us through His death on the cross!

1 Peter 5:6 KJVS

[6] Humble yourselves therefore under the mighty hand of God, that he may exalt you in due time:

Now because gifts carry innately the spirit of humility, they have the ability and right from God to be exalted. Because they have paid the price of humility and came down to earth in order to serve The Lord, they can be exalted by God at any time! This is the mystery of gifts on the earth. They can be exalted at any time because of *their* humility, but the person to whom they are given must be disciplined enough to wait for the *time of exaltation* from the Father (Galatians 4:2). This is what Jesus did in His life when He went to be baptized by John the Baptist, He knew the time of His exaltation from the Father.

Many times today especially in Christianity and in ministry, men and women do not wait for the time of exaltation from The Father. They unknowingly allow the humility of their gift to cause them to be exalted before time, but it's not them being exalted, it's the gift in them being exalted by God. You see the gift in you is prepared to *wait* until the time of your exaltation from the Father. It's us who are not willing to wait, to be humbled, processed, and then exalted by God.

This is why many men and women in the body of Christ have risen to prominence and become well known, but they weren't processed enough to last, therefore they fell. They allowed the gift in them to be exalted when they themselves were not ready to be exalted. Their character was not ready to walk through the doors and stand in the rooms that their gifts opened and made for them. This is how your gift can be light while you yet walk in darkness. This issue has caused much damage to the Body of Christ in the past. Now God is moving to fix this reoccurring issue by revealing the true nature of gifts and the maturity that needs to be developed in us to steward them with longevity and not fall short due to a lack of process!

Knowledge or God

Many believers today have no idea of this ancient battle and warfare within them that is taking place. The battle between knowledge and God. This is the most ancient battle since the beginning of the generations of Adam. In the garden God commanded Adam and Eve not to eat of the tree of the knowledge of good and evil, but they disobeyed him. Since then, the battle between knowledge and God has been raging inside of mankind and is still raging today.

Genesis 2:17 KJVS

*[17] But of the **tree of the knowledge of good and evil, thou shalt not eat of it**: for in the day that thou eatest thereof thou shalt surely die.*

Mankind's spirit, soul, and body began to die or the process of dying the day Adam and Eve disobeyed God. The reason they died was because they chose a life source that was not everlasting. The tree of life was everlasting in life. Which is why after Adam and Eve fell they had to be removed from the garden. God did not want them to have access to the tree of life and live forever in a sinful state of being.

Genesis 3:22-24 KJVS

*[22] And the Lord God said, Behold, the man is become as one of us, **to know good and evil: and now, lest he put forth his hand, and take also of the tree of life, and eat, and live for***

*ever: [23] **Therefore the Lord God sent him forth from the garden of Eden**, to till the ground from whence he was taken. [24] **So he drove out the man; and he placed at the east of the garden of Eden Cherubims, and a flaming sword which turned every way, to keep the way of the tree of life.***

Before Adam and Eve fell their primary focus and purpose was to know God! Good and evil were irrelevant to them because they walked in a higher realm, where evil did not exist in them or to them. They walked in what the Bible calls *the more excellent way* in 1 Corinthians 12:31, *which is love*. We know that God is love, they walked in God and God walked in them. They were not called to know evil but to know everlasting life in God!

But since that time there has been an ever growing and seemingly insatiable desire for *knowledge* in mankind. This is what consumes mankind. We have an inherent taste of the tree of the knowledge of good and evil in us from Adam and Eve that must be overcome by love for God.

Ephesians 3:19 KJVS

[19] And to know the love of Christ, which passeth knowledge, that ye might be filled with all the fulness of God.

You see, it's the love of Christ that passes knowledge! And in order for us to be filled with the fullness of God we must pass knowledge also. The truth is we will either be filled with knowledge or filled with God in His fullness. Satan is using this same strategy that he used with Eve in the beginning. Which is the lure and temptation of knowledge. But this is not the knowledge of God but the carnal knowledge of good and evil. He made her feel like God was withholding information or knowledge from her and she fell for it. But knowledge did increase in them because instantly they knew they were naked and hid themselves. But once again, this was not the knowledge of God. So we must ask ourselves, what is Satan stealing from you with this strategy? *Time!* Think about it, if you spend the majority of your life seeking the knowledge of good and evil, how much time do you have for getting to know God? Not much at all.

You will either have the testimony of man (carnality) or have the testimony of God. This will be based on what you are determined to *know* in your lifetime. The more you know about mankind or others, the less you will know about God and vice versa. It is all about what you desire or determine to know, one will excel and one will suffer. Satan's goal is for us to waste our God given lives being gluttons for the knowledge of good and evil. This is why we can't put our phones down and we spend hours scrolling. It is because it has become our source of food (substance/nourishment) that feeds our souls. We crave the knowledge of good and evil and not the knowledge of God which comes from the tree of life! The news, social media, blogs, vlogs, tabloids, magazines and reality tv, all of these mediums feed us the knowledge of good and evil and saturate our appetites and cravings for them. We must be determined *not to know*, if we're going to know God! We must be determined not to know if God doesn't tell us. This will literally feel like *fasting* for those of us weening ourselves off of the knowledge of good and evil.

You can tell what tree a person is eating from by their appetite (their taste and cravings). If all they crave is gossip and information about others. If this consumes the vast majority of their lives. Then they are definitely consuming their nourishment from the tree of the knowledge of good and evil. It is actually knowledge that hinders forgiveness. We struggle to forgive people because of what *we know* about them or our knowledge of them. We say "I *know* what kind of person they are" or "You don't *know* what they did to me." It's all knowledge! But Christ's Love passes knowledge or loves beyond knowledge. Jesus doesn't allow any knowledge He has, whether good or bad, to change the way He feels about us. That's what we do, we allow what we know or find out about people to change the way we feel about them, but that's not true love! This is the reason people hide or lie about certain things in their lives, because they fear people getting certain knowledge about them, because they know it will change the way people feel about them. And that people as a result of that knowledge will judge and criticize them. This is not the Way of The Lord, but the Way of The Lord is love and life! Love covers others, it doesn't expose people unnecessarily because of feelings and emotions about them.

Proverbs 10:12 KJVS

[12] Hatred stirreth up strifes: **but love covereth all sins.**

Proverbs 17:9 KJVS

[9] **He that covereth a transgression seeketh love;** *but he that*

repeateth a matter separateth very friends.

God desires a people to be led by love! He wants people who are hungry to know Him, and He is Love! To know God is to know true love and love is enough. If God doesn't reveal certain information (knowledge) to you it is because He has not deemed it as important for you to know. We through our relationship with God have to trust His Heart and reasonings (ways) on why He does things the way He does them. We need trust that His Ways are indeed higher than our ways and His thoughts higher than our thoughts (Isaiah 55:9). Our lives should be totally given to knowing God and all that He is!

1 Corinthians 2:2 KJVS

*[2] **For I determined not to know any thing among you,** save Jesus Christ, and him crucified.*

WHEN THE LIGHT HITS THE WATER

There is a mystery in the spirit of man between the light of God's Word and the water within the spirit of the believer. Our Lord Jesus released a mystery of the spirit of man and spoke of it as being the *belly* or the center of a being.

John 7:38-39 KJVS

*[38] He that believeth on me, as the scripture hath said, out of his belly shall flow **rivers of living water.** [39] (But this spake he of the Spirit, which they that believe on him should receive: for the Holy Ghost was not yet given ; because that Jesus was not yet glorified.)*

We see in this passage of scripture that when the Spirit of God is received by a believer in Christ Jesus, our spirit becomes filled with rivers of living water.

1 Corinthians 6:17 KJVS

[17] But he that is joined unto the Lord is one spirit.

When we are baptized in the Holy Spirit our spirit man becomes one with God through the Holy Spirit. The Holy Spirit is not just a Person being God, but He created and holds a *world* within Himself called the Kingdom of God.

Romans 14:17 KJVS

*[17] For the kingdom of God is not meat and drink; but righteousness, and peace, and joy **in the Holy Ghost.***

Luke 17:21 KJVS

*[21] Neither shall they say, Lo here! or, lo there! for, behold, **the kingdom of God is within you.***

So according to scripture the Kingdom of God dwells within every Spirit-filled believer. Which brings us to the revelation of *the light hitting the water.*

Revelation 4:6 KJVS

*[6] And before the throne there was a **sea of glass like unto crystal...***

This passage of scripture gives us a revelation of something that is within the Kingdom of God, which is a *sea of glass.* Within our spirit there is a sea of glass before which the Throne of GOD that is within us. What is significant about this revelation is that water is *reflective!* We all know that in the natural realm we can see our reflection in water, but this came from the Kingdom of God and is still in the Kingdom of God.

When the light of God's glory proceeding from His throne hits the sea of glass (water), it reflects the true state and reality of the people standing on the sea.

Revelation 4:2 KJVS

*[2] And immediately I was **in the spirit**: and, behold, **a throne was set in heaven, and one sat on the throne.***

Revelation 22:5 KJVS

*[5] And there shall be no night there; and they need no candle, neither light of the sun; **for the Lord God giveth them light**: and they shall reign for ever and ever.*

Revelation 15:2 KJVS

*[2] And I saw as it were a **sea of glass** mingled with fire: **and***

them that had gotten the victory over the beast, and over his image, and over his mark, and over the number of his name, stand on the sea of glass, having the harps of God.

This sea of glass reveals to us who we *really are!* We see our purified state of eternal being through the fire on this sea of glass, *it is the Father's Vision of us! The Truth of who we really are!* The overcomers in heaven see the reflection of the image of God in themselves. They see the state of being God always intended them to live in, and this reflection of God in themselves causes them to fall down before the Throne of God and worship Him for His Everlasting Goodness toward us! Seeing He has made us with such glory and splendor, that we are *indeed* the image of the Glorious God!

This mystery of the Light hitting the water within us, not only takes place in eternity, but also in the here and now. And it comes through the written and spoken Word of God.

Psalm 119:130 KJVS

[130] The **entrance of thy words giveth light***; it giveth understanding unto the simple.*

When we read the Word of GOD with an open heart, the light of the word enters into our spirit man and shines on the living water within us and reflects our current condition, good, bad or ugly. We have to be both humble and willing to acknowledge the truth about us that is reflected by the light of God's Word. The Spirit of God (Living Waters) reflects what is on the inside of you, to you! We must acknowledge and not teach our hearts to lie and deceive ourselves, through pride and denial. But we draw from the wells within us, which are called *wells of salvation* and drink the living truth and allow it to wash and cleanse our lives.

Isaiah 12:3 KJVS

[3] Therefore **with joy shall ye draw water out of the wells of salvation.**

The scripture here tells what type of spirit or attitude we're supposed to have when drawing from the wells of salvation, which is joy! This is because these *wells of salvation* are solidifying and securing your place in God for eternity. This happens in a much deeper way than we can yet realize. They are literally *wells of salvation, wells of living water that saves the souls of all those who drink and bathe in them.*

So allow the Light of God's Word to shine within you reflecting off of the Living Waters of Life. Allow the truth that is revealed to set you free from sin, the flesh, and wickedness. The Living Waters inside you are indeed the wells of Salvation (Deliverance) reflecting the Light of His Word revealing truth to you, to set you free! It is not only to set you free from evil, but to bless you with good! Remember James' statement in his letter in the Bible:

James 1:23-25 KJVS

*[23] For if any be a hearer of the word, and not a doer, **he is like unto a man beholding his natural face in a glass:** [24] For **he beholdeth himself,** and goeth his way, **and straightway forgetteth what manner of man he was.** [25] But whoso looketh into the perfect law of liberty, and continueth therein, he being not a forgetful hearer, but **a doer of the work, this man shall be blessed in his deed.***

CONCLUSION

As we come to the end of this book, we've taken a spiritual journey into prayer, mysteries and relationship with God. My hope is that you've learned strategies in prayer to get answers and breakthrough. That our dives into mysteries of the Kingdom have enlightened you and caused you to have a greater understanding of the ways of The Lord. Ultimately that your relationship with The Lord has been ignited into a deeper level of intimacy and desire!

In conclusion I pray that this book will fulfill the prayer of the Apostle Paul in Ephesians 1:17-18! That this would be your impartation from the words of this book and forever more!

> *Ephesians 1:17-19 KJVS*
>
> *[17] That the God of our Lord Jesus Christ, the Father of glory, may give unto you the spirit of wisdom and revelation in the knowledge of him: [18] The eyes of your understanding being enlightened; that ye may know what is the hope of his calling, and what the riches of the glory of his inheritance in the saints, [19] And what is the exceeding greatness of his power to us-ward who believe, according to the working of his mighty power,*

About the Author

Paige Michael Williams is a minister of the Gospel of Jesus Christ from northeast Ohio. God speaks to him by revelation through dreams and visions, as well as prophetically. In 2017 He was given a commission by The Lord to "Write down what you hear." This book is just a small fulfillment of that commission.

SeraphCreative

Heaven's Heart for Earth

Seraph Creative is a collective of artists, writers, theologians & illustrators who desire to see the body of Christ grow into full maturity, walking in their inheritance as Sons of God on the Earth.

Sign up to our newsletter to know about future exciting releases.

Visit our website :

www.seraphcreative.org

www.ingramcontent.com/pod-product-compliance
Lightning Source LLC
Chambersburg PA
CBHW051550120626
46551CB00013B/1447